Write like you'
out of time

there's a million things I haven't done...
But just you wait, just you wait

★

I am not throwing away my shot

Raise a glass to Freedom
Something they can never take away

Love doesn't discriminate
between the sinners and the saints

Look around, look around at how lucky we are to be alive right now

_____
_____
_____
_____
_____
_____
_____
_____
_____
_____
_____
_____
_____
_____
_____
_____
_____
_____
_____
_____
_____
_____
_____
_____
_____
_____

I wrote my way out of hell
I wrote my way to revolution

History has its eyes on you

Work! Work!

Rise up!

What is a legacy? It's planting seeds in a garden you'll never see.

★

I am inimitable.
I am an original.

Pssst! We have a secret offer!

Do you belong to a group or club that would love its very
own workbooks? We can create custom journals,
notebooks & sketchbooks just for YOU!
No design charge. Unlimited books.

Interested? Drop us a line at:

PembrokePublishing@gmail.com

Made in the USA
Columbia, SC
16 December 2020